First Chinese Words

Illustrated by David Melling

OXFORD

UNIVERSITY PRESS

For Bosiljka, Branko and Igor Sunajko.
D.M.

OXFORD
UNIVERSITY PRESS

Great Clarendon Street, Oxford OX2 6DP

Oxford University Press is a department of the University of Oxford.
It furthers the University's objective of excellence in research, scholarship,
and education by publishing worldwide in

Oxford   New York

Auckland   Cape Town   Dar es Salaam   Hong Kong   Karachi
Kuala Lumpur   Madrid   Melbourne   Mexico City   Nairobi
New Delhi   Shanghai   Taipei   Toronto

With offices in

Argentina   Austria   Brazil   Chile   Czech Republic   France   Greece
Guatemala   Hungary   Italy   Japan   Poland   Portugal   Singapore
South Korea   Switzerland   Thailand   Turkey   Ukraine   Vietnam

Oxford is a registered trade mark of Oxford University Press
in the UK and in certain other countries

Illustrations copyright © David Melling 1999
Text copyright © Oxford University Press 1999

Database right Oxford University Press (maker)

First published as First Book of Words in hardback 1999
First published in paperback 2000
First published as First Chinese Words 2009

English words compiled by Neil Morris
Chinese translation by Yuen Chan

British Library Cataloguing in Publication Data available

ISBN: 978-0-19-911205-0
1 3 5 7 9 10 8 6 4 2

Paper used in the production of this book is a natural,
recyclable product made from wood grown in sustainable forests.
The manufacturing process conforms to the environmental
regulations of the country of origin.

Printed in Singapore

All efforts have been made to ensure that these translations are
accurate and appropriate. If you have any further language queries,
please visit our website at www.askoxford.com.

Contents

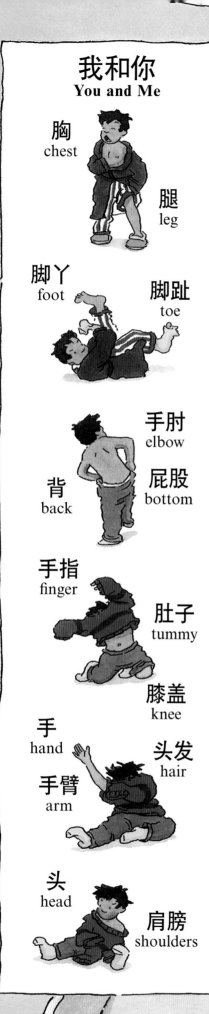

我和你
You and Me

胸
chest

腿
leg

脚丫
foot

脚趾
toe

手肘
elbow

背
back

屁股
bottom

手指
finger

肚子
tummy

膝盖
knee

手
hand

头发
hair

手臂
arm

头
head

肩膀
shoulders

脸
face

脸蛋
cheek

耳朵
ear

眼睛
eye

下巴
chin

嘴巴
mouth

牙齿
teeth

舌头
tongue

脖子
neck

鼻子
nose

女孩
girl

男孩
boy

我的家
At Home

屋顶
roof

垃圾桶
dustbin/(US) trashcan

闸门
gate

楼梯
stairs

烟囱
chimney

栅栏
fence

车库
garage

窗
window

门
door

狗
dog

猫
cat

兔子
rabbit

蜘蛛
spider

蜗牛
snail

信件
letters

邮袋
postbag

叶子
leaf

花
flower

树
tree

上学去
On the Way to School

路灯柱
lamp post

人行道
pavement

操场
playground

马路
street

斑马线
zebra crossing/
(US) crosswalk

学校
school

红绿灯
traffic lights

店铺
shop

教堂
church

8

单车
bicycle

车子
car

巴士
bus

摩托车
motorbike

消防车
fire engine

卡车
truck

直升机
helicopter

救护车
ambulance

飞机
plane

我们的教室
Our Classroom

书包
school bag

饭盒
lunch box

书
book

黑板
blackboard

粉笔
chalk

地球仪
globe

书桌
desk

磁铁
magnet

果皮箱
bin

10

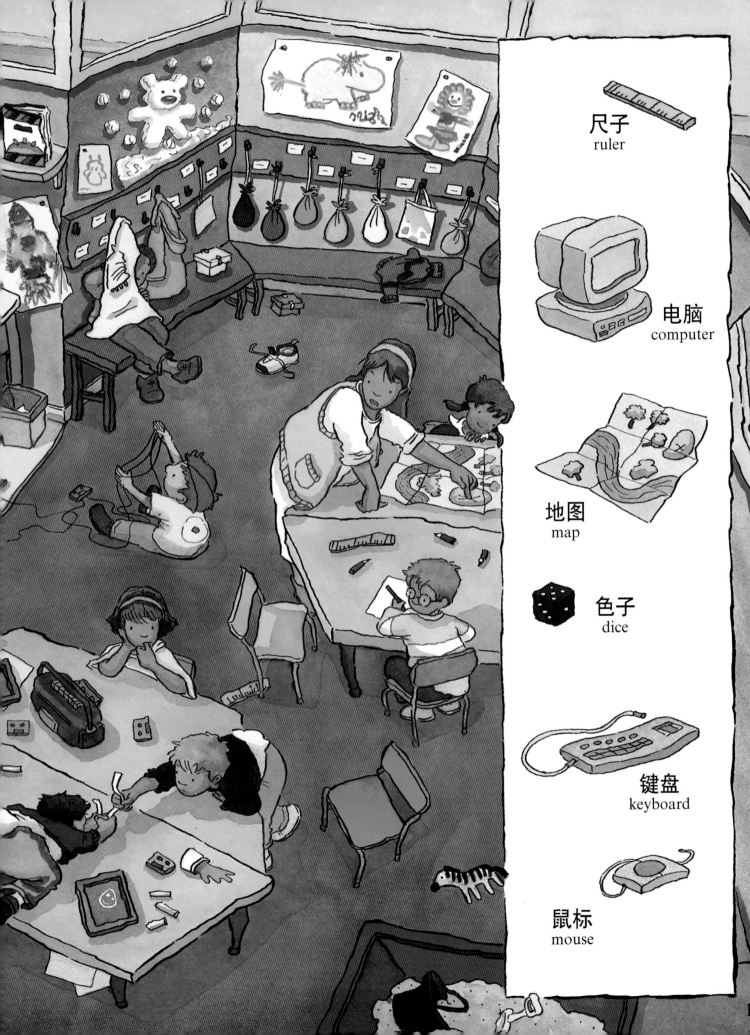

尺子
ruler

电脑
computer

地图
map

色子
dice

键盘
keyboard

鼠标
mouse

11

好玩的色彩
Fun with Colours

黑色
black

蓝色
blue

棕色
brown

绿色
green

灰色
grey

橙色
orange

粉红色
pink

紫色
purple

红色
red

白色
white

黄色
yellow

围裙
overalls

胶水
glue

画
painting

画笔
paintbrush

油漆
paints

铅笔
pencil

纸张
paper

剪刀
scissors

彩笔
felt-tip pen

画架
easel

13

各行各业
Professions

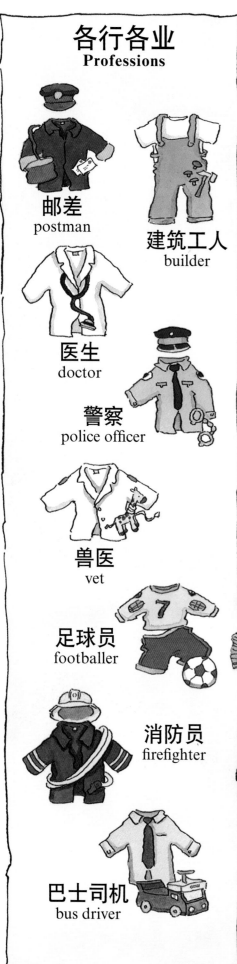

邮差
postman

建筑工人
builder

医生
doctor

警察
police officer

兽医
vet

足球员
footballer

消防员
firefighter

巴士司机
bus driver

火车司机
train driver

歌星
pop star

飞行员
pilot

舞蹈员
dancer

潜水员
diver

厨师
cook

太空人
astronaut

救生员
lifeguard

15

很久以前
Long Time Ago

恐龙
Dinosaurs

二亿年前
200 million years ago

暴龙
Tyrannosaurus Rex

剑龙
Stegosaurus

梁龙
Diplodocus

三角龙骨骼
Triceratops skeleton

化石
fossil

骨头
bone

石器时代的人类
Stone Age Man
一万年前
10,000 years ago

山洞
cave

火石
flint

洞穴壁画
cave painting

火
fire

古埃及人
Ancient Egyptians
五千年前
5,000 years ago

金字塔
pyramid

法老王
Pharaoh

狮身人面像
Sphinx

古罗马人
Ancient Romans
二千年前
2,000 years ago

陶器
pottery

士兵
soldier

钱币
coins

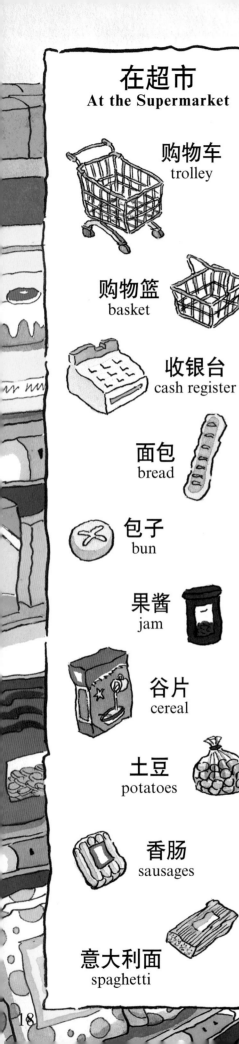

在超市
At the Supermarket

购物车
trolley

购物篮
basket

收银台
cash register

面包
bread

包子
bun

果酱
jam

谷片
cereal

土豆
potatoes

香肠
sausages

意大利面
spaghetti

牛奶
milk

酸奶
yoghurt

奶酪
cheese

鸡蛋
eggs

苹果
apple

香蕉
banana

橙子
orange

西红柿
tomato

胡萝卜
carrot

生菜
lettuce

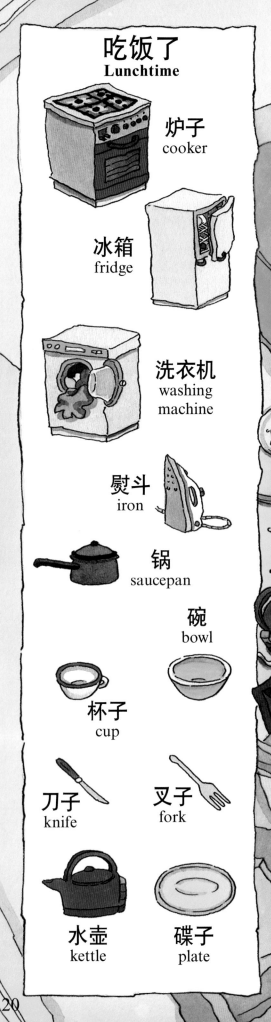

吃饭了
Lunchtime

炉子
cooker

冰箱
fridge

洗衣机
washing
machine

熨斗
iron

锅
saucepan

碗
bowl

杯子
cup

刀子
knife

叉子
fork

水壶
kettle

碟子
plate

勺子
spoon

小碟子
saucer

椅子
chair

茶壶
teapot

垫子
cushion

沙发
sofa

唱机
stereo

桌子
table

电视
television

吸尘机
vacuum cleaner

21

玩吧
Playtime

玩具屋
doll's house

娃娃
doll

游戏
game

赛车
racing car

机器人
robot

拼图
jigsaw puzzle

泰迪熊
teddy

玩具火车
train set

22

鼓
drum

吉他
guitar

电子琴
keyboard

麦克风
microphone

喇叭
trumpet

竖笛
recorder

钹子
cymbals

手铃
bells

铃鼓
tambourine

23

在农场
On the Farm

马
horse

鸡
chicken

公鸡
cockerel

鸭子
duck

鹅
goose

绵羊
sheep

羚羊
goat

猪
pig

牛
cow

24

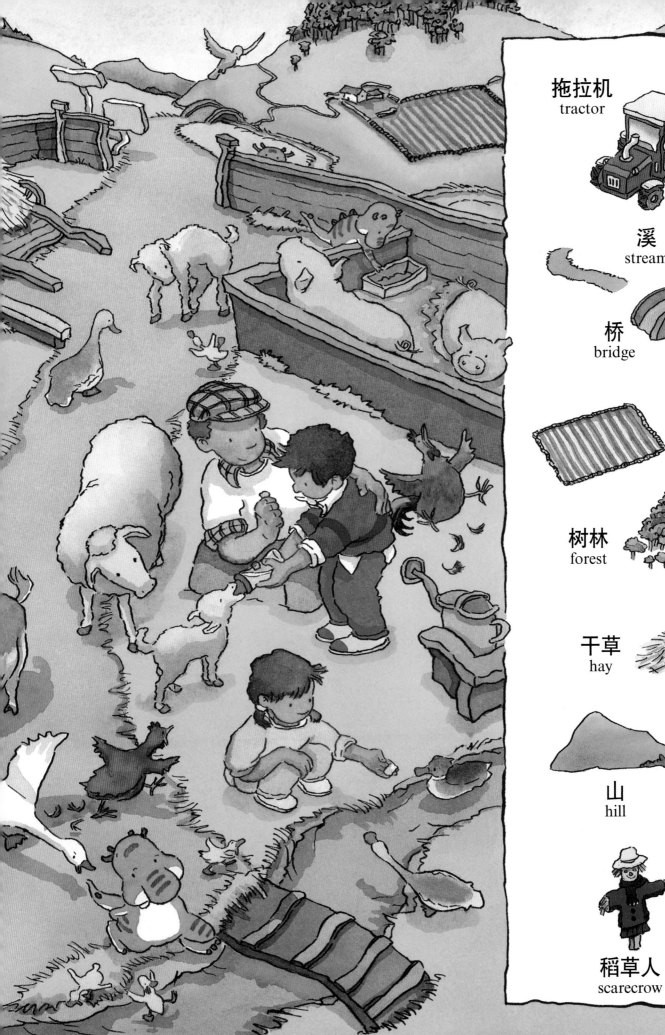

拖拉机
tractor

溪
stream

桥
bridge

田
field

树林
forest

干草
hay

山
hill

稻草人
scarecrow

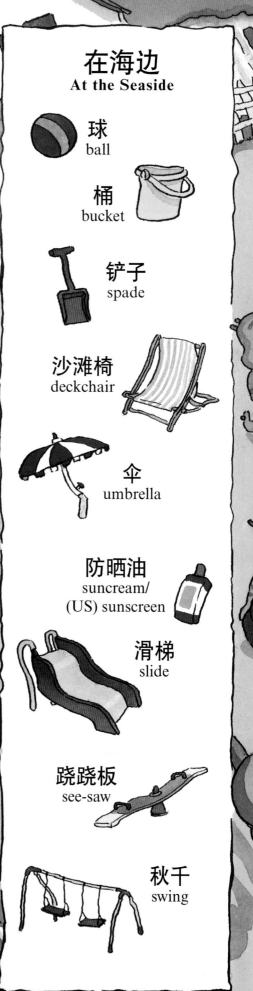

在海边
At the Seaside

球
ball

桶
bucket

铲子
spade

沙滩椅
deckchair

伞
umbrella

防晒油
suncream/
(US) sunscreen

滑梯
slide

跷跷板
see-saw

秋千
swing

船
ship

灯塔
lighthouse

沙堡
sandcastle

海鸥
seagull

贝壳
shell

螃蟹
crab

八爪鱼
octopus

海星
starfish

海带
seaweed

生日会
Birthday Party

生日卡
birthday card

蜡烛
candle

气球
balloon

礼物
present

彩带
streamer

吹吹卷
party blower

玩具帽
party hat

魔杖
wand

魔术师
magician

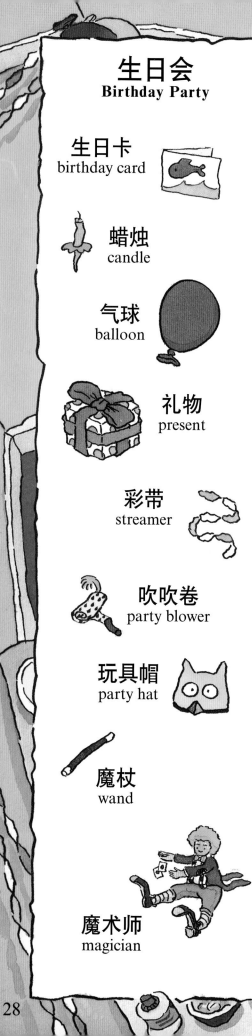

28

糖果
sweets

三明治
sandwich

披萨饼
pizza

冰淇淋
ice cream

巧克力
chocolate

饼干
biscuit

吸管
straw

饮料
drink

蛋糕
cake

有趣的动物
Amusing Animals

大象
elephant

鳄鱼
crocodile

长颈鹿
giraffe

鱼
fish

河马
hippopotamus

袋鼠
kangaroo

猴子
monkey

考拉熊
koala

老鼠
mouse

海象
walrus

鹦鹉
parrot

企鹅
penguin

老虎
tiger

斑马
zebra

熊猫
panda

羚牛
rhinoceros

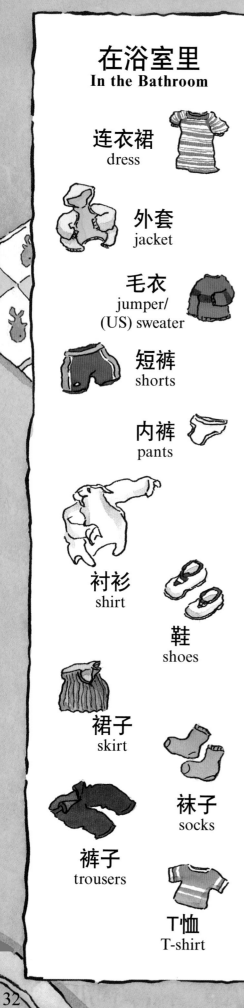

在浴室里
In the Bathroom

连衣裙
dress

外套
jacket

毛衣
jumper/
(US) sweater

短裤
shorts

内裤
pants

衬衫
shirt

鞋
shoes

裙子
skirt

袜子
socks

裤子
trousers

T恤
T-shirt

洗脸盘
basin

浴缸
bath

小毛巾
flannel

镜子
mirror

淋浴器
shower

肥皂
soap

海绵
sponge

厕所
toilet

卫生纸
toilet paper

牙刷
toothbrush

牙膏
toothpaste

毛巾
towel

晚安！
Goodnight!

衣柜
wardrobe

窗帘
curtains

床头柜
bedside table

台灯
lamp

睡裙
nightdress

睡衣
pyjamas

枕头
pillow

床
bed

毛毯
blanket

柜子
chest

故事书
storybook

城堡
castle

国王
king

王后
queen

灯神
genie

神灯
magic lamp

龙
dragon

巨人
giant

35

我的图片字典
My Picture Dictionary

Match the words with the pictures

蚂蚁
ant

蛋
egg

鱼
fish

铃
bell

直升机
helicopter

狗
dog

杂耍演员
juggler

国王
king

王后
queen

八爪鱼
octopus

小货车
van

瓢虫
ladybird

木偶
puppet

老鼠
mouse

钉子
nail

毛虫
caterpillar

伞
umbrella

戒指
ring

X光
x-ray

游艇
yacht

袜子
socks

老虎
tiger

墨水
ink

手表
watch

斑马
zebra

山羊
goat

跟我一起数数！123
Count with Me! 123

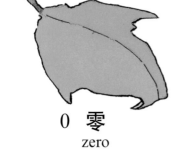 0 零
zero

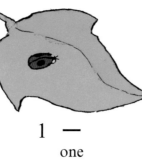 1 一
one

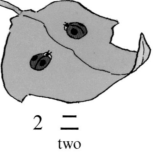 2 二
two

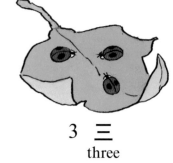 3 三
three

 4 四
four

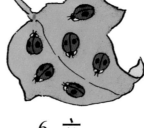 5 五
five

 6 六
six

 7 七
seven

 8 八
eight

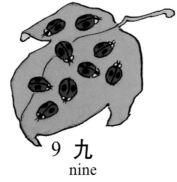 9 九
nine

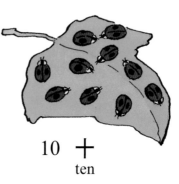 10 十
ten

第一
first

第二
second

第三
third

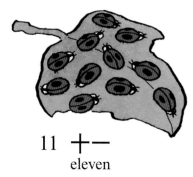

11 十一
eleven

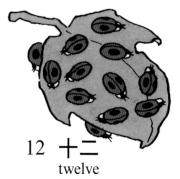

12 十二
twelve

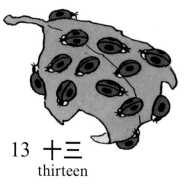

13 十三
thirteen

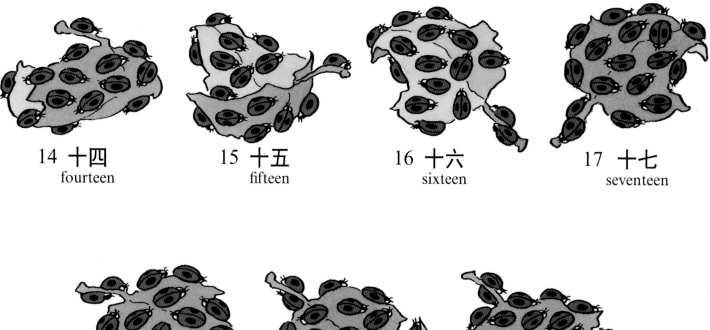

14 十四
fourteen

15 十五
fifteen

16 十六
sixteen

17 十七
seventeen

18 十八
eighteen

19 十九
nineteen

20 二十
twenty

第四
fourth

第五
fifth

最后
last

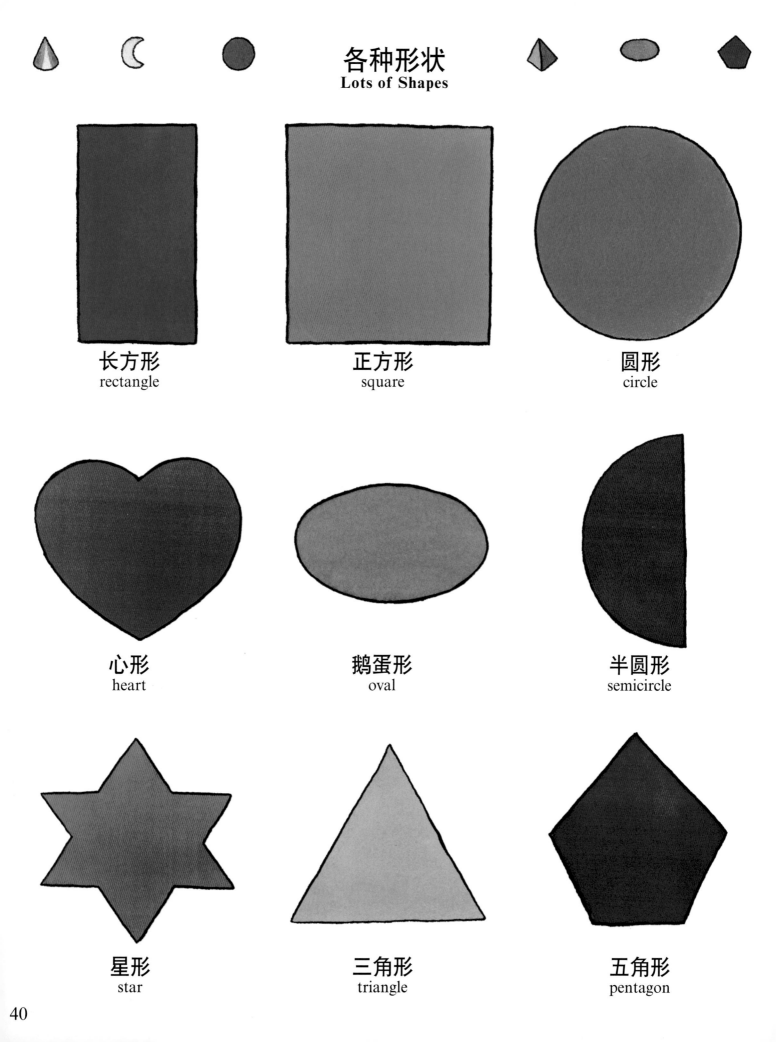

各种形状
Lots of Shapes

长方形
rectangle

正方形
square

圆形
circle

心形
heart

鹅蛋形
oval

半圆形
semicircle

星形
star

三角形
triangle

五角形
pentagon

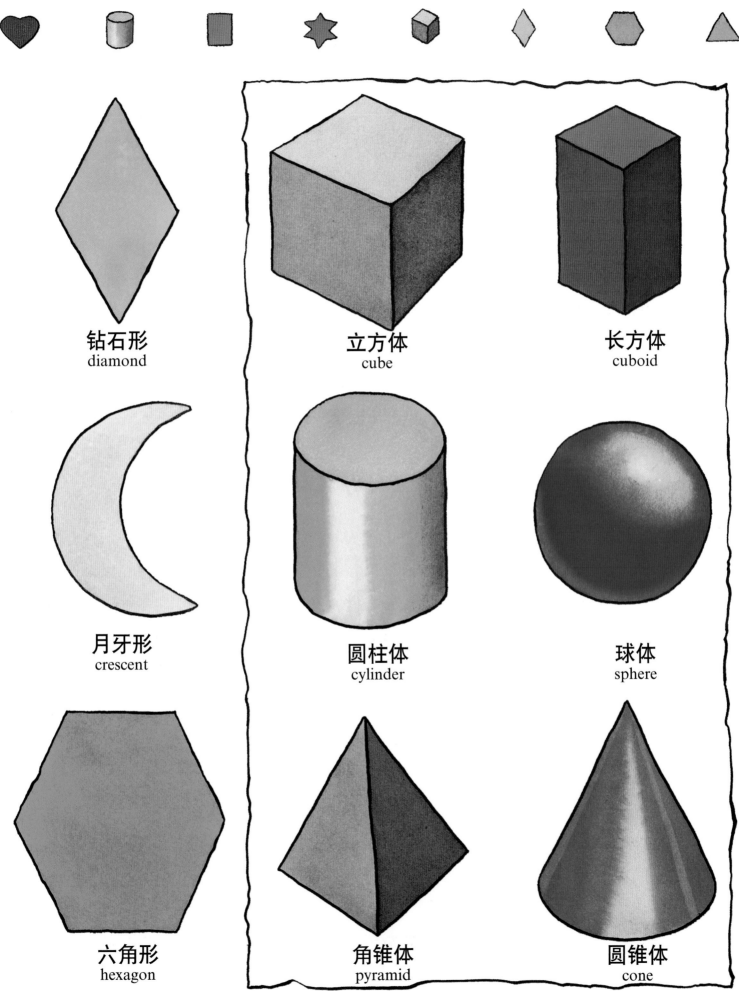

钻石形
diamond

立方体
cube

长方体
cuboid

月牙形
crescent

圆柱体
cylinder

球体
sphere

六角形
hexagon

角锥体
pyramid

圆锥体
cone

41

相反
Opposites

大/小
big/small

干净/脏
clean/dirty

胖/瘦
fat/thin

满/空
full/empty

高/低
high/low

热/冷
hot/cold

新/旧
new/old

开/关
open/closed

暗／亮
dark/light

快／慢
fast/slow

乐／悲
happy/sad

重／轻
heavy/light

长／短
long/short

多／少
more/less

一样／不一样
same/different

湿／干
wet/dry

43

天气
Weather

阴天
cloudy

晴天
sunny

下雨
rainy

下雪
snowy

刮风
windy

雾蒙蒙
foggy

八点钟
eight o'clock

十点钟
ten o'clock

十二点钟
twelve o'clock

两点钟
two o'clock

四点钟
four o'clock

六点钟
six o'clock

Index